FEMENISMO

T0273329

Joanne Limburg was born in London in 1970, and studied Philosophy at Cambridge. She has since gained an MA in Psychoanalytic Studies, worked as an Associate Lecturer for the Open University, and was the Royal Literary Fund Fellow at Magdalen College, Cambridge, from 2008 to 2010. She won an Eric Gregory Award for her poetry in 1998, and her first book, *Femenismo* (Bloodaxe Books, 2000), was shortlisted for the Forward Prize for Best First Collection. Her second collection, *Paraphernalia* (Bloodaxe Books, 2007), was a Poetry Book Society Recommendation. Her third, *The Autistic Alice*, was published by Bloodaxe in 2017.

Her other books include *The Woman Who Thought Too Much* (Atlantic Books, 2010), a memoir about OCD, anxiety and poetry; *Bookside Down: poems for the modern, discerning cyber-kid* (Salt Publishing, 2013), an anthology for younger readers; her novel *A Want of Kindness: a novel of Queen Anne* (Atlantic Books, 2015); and *Letters to my Weird Sisters: On Autism and Feminism* (Atlantic Books, 2021).

JOANNE LIMBURG

◈

Femenismo

BLOODAXE BOOKS

Copyright © Joanne Limburg 2000

ISBN: 978 1 85224 540 5

First published 2000 by
Bloodaxe Books Ltd,
Eastburn,
South Park,
Hexham,
Northumberland NE46 1BS.

www.bloodaxebooks.com
For further information about Bloodaxe titles
please visit our website and join our mailing list
or write to the above address for a catalogue.

Supported using public funding by
ARTS COUNCIL
ENGLAND

Digital reprint of the 2000 Bloodaxe Books edition.

i.m.

Maurice Derek Limburg

1934–1996

ACKNOWLEDGEMENTS

Acknowledgements are due to the editors of the following publications in which some of these poems first appeared: *Dandelion Arts Magazine, ibid, The Interpreter's House, Iota, New Blood* (Bloodaxe Books, 1999), *The North, Obsessed with Pipework, Other Poetry, Perceptions, Poetry Nottingham International, Psychopoetica, Smiths Knoll, Southfields, Thumbscrew* and *The Wide Skirt*.

I would like to thank the Society of Authors and their judges for granting me an Eric Gregory Award in 1998.

Also thanks to: my teachers; Sarah, Sheila, Nasim, Warner, Helen, Florence, Patricia, Liz and Chris; my family, especially Lisa.

CONTENTS

An After-Life

It's the usual second post:
a museum catalogue, two charity appeals
and a message from the other side,
this time in a C5 envelope,
manilla, with a window.

Sometimes it's an A4, or foolscap,
sometimes there's a stick-on label
but the message inside
is always the same:

He is not dead.

They have saved him onto disk
and even now
pulsing through some circuit
are the bytes, the letters
of his indestructible name
become all energy, all light,
and rising again
with every mail merge.

And if I thought for one moment
that there was not an after-life,
it must have been
that I was swayed by appearances:
by the thud of earth on his coffin
or by the snapping of his credit cards
like the plastic crack of doom.

My Family Fly South

My family take off together,
flying south like a feathered arrow
pointing the way so that nobody
should forget.

My family believe in flocking together:
we're so alike we use each other
as mirrors, and for a crystal ball
I use my mother.

Pecking in the fields together,
my family squabble for corn and attention,
bringing every meal to an end
with a good row.

My family stick together
if attacked by outsiders. Setting our beaks
towards them, we flap our wings and launch
a united squawk.

My family plot a course together:
nothing else makes sense. We shout
after children who try to leave: *You won't
get far on your own!*

Travelling Light

Never underestimate
the ecstasy of chucking out:

the clean desktop, the orderly wardrobe,
the black bags stacked by the shut front door,

the softness of a shaven calf,
the bracing soreness of the friction glove –

a text that could edit itself would know it,
linen being boiled must know it,

that godly joy of cleanliness,
the pleasure of being stripped bare

and blameless, a born-again
with just one suitcase, on the right road.

Curse

Good luck is like old money.
I was born into it
and wear it like a shrug.

They hated me at school,
me and my complete set
of cigarette cards,
me and my full deck
of impeccable 'A's.
They never let me join in.
They said it was boring,
the way I'd always win.

They never knew
how hard I tried to lose,
Saturday mornings letting my luck slip
into skips and pushchairs
and people's supermarket trolleys,
only to turn
and find it trailing behind
like a mitten on a string.

I never found a way
to stop it showing.
Everywhere I go,
people stop to admire
my golden shadow.
They say how wonderful,
I've got everything going for me.
Then I hear them muttering
behind my back.

And all I want to do
is sit around like them in bars and cafés,
blaming my lack of it.

Among Her People

The Princess is slumming it.
She doesn't remember
how she fell from her feather bed
onto hard times

but she knows she displays
all the signs of her origins
such as tapering fingers
and no common sense.

She pities the wretches
who slave for the Government,
accepts her benefit cheque
as their tribute

and when she's restored
to her rightful position,
she'll pardon the subjects
who've pushed her in bus queues.

A Medieval Life

As most of her writings were burned
(by her), there's little left to shed light
on a life spent in her skin, but it's
enough to make mine crawl: purges,

fasts, horrific blood-lettings,
the knotted cord she used to whip
herself, her endless bargaining
with the supernatural, her prayers:

O Lord, I know I am the least,
the lowest, the weakest of all souls,
but I beg you, lend me the strength
to suffer, to cleanse myself for you.

I couldn't begin to understand her,
or to picture the distance between us,
that untraceable leap from her
hot magic to my cool psychology.

The First Fruit Salad

One June night
she left her husband sleeping
in the record-breaking heat
and went down to ask the fridge
what it was she wanted.

What she wanted was:
the life of a fruiteater,
an endless afternoon
in a cool and juicy place
where white teeth sank into Spanish oranges
and apples fell open into perfect halves
on wooden chopping-boards,
all by themselves, all day,
and cubes of watermelon
clinked in long glasses.

Splay-legged on the kitchen floor,
she hugged the bowl of fruit salad
to her chest, and remembered how,
at the very beginning,
Eve sat, blindfold and giggling,
as he brought the spoonfuls up to her mouth,
one by one,
to be named.

The Queen of Swords

Every few weeks or so, I make
an appointment with this woman to tidy
my head up and trim my ends. It's risky.
On my way in, I often pass

some of her other clients holding
bloody rags to ears or necks –
she frequently forgets herself
in her eagerness to do you good.

But I'm not scared of the sharp gleam
in her eye when she tells me what
my problem is. It's the sign of the clearest
eyesight, a diamond of a mind.

To the Bride, from Her Best Friend

As there's no ceremony
to join two friends,
I've made one up for us.

First of all,
we'll vow to keep the faith
by slagging off all others,
blaming our faults on our mothers
and never ever
telling the waiter
what it is we're laughing at.

Then, we'll drink a toast.
To me,
for my boldness
in wearing coloured tights.
To you,
for the way you've inspired me
with your genius for panic.

Then, we'll exchange gifts.
You can have my self-control,
that you're so in awe of,
that I'm so sick of.
I'll take your sexual allure
(well, you won't need it any more).

And then, for the last time,
we'll shut the door
on that messy room,
the accumulated flotsam of eight years:
textbooks and headaches,
coffee mugs, chocolate wrappers,
abandoned skins.

A Lesson in Ballooning

First of all – the instructor said –
we should forget the myth we'd learned
in school that only the best could fly.

Quite the opposite was true
and by the end of the morning everyone
in that room would rediscover

her God-given power to leave the ground.
He smiled at us, a nodding circle
of earnest girls in ethnic skirts,

split us into groups of four
and took the lid off his marker pen.
I admit I was sceptical at first:

the uplifting quotes I could take or leave,
the hugging just embarrassed me
but then, quite abruptly – just before coffee –

I felt the ground release my feet...
...and I was up with a rush of air:
easy as stepping out of a shoe

to shed the room, the building, the street
and rise until the London I'd left
was just a teeming *A-Z*.

The city's asthmatic wheeze grew faint
as I breathed in the pure, blue
laughing gas of almost-heaven.

Dusk fell. I drifted lazily
over the green belt. Then I discovered
that I couldn't feel my toes;

had slipped, quite gently, out of my skin
like a tomato in boiling water.
At once I was vomiting sunset

as if I were a spoilt birthday
girl, puking up the trifle.
The whole of the sky was my head and it ached.

Suddenly I was nostalgic for ceilings,
yearning for home, with all its walls
and for someone to break my upward fall.

The Tube Ministry

Our preacher for today gets on
at Willesden Green and instantly
I prove myself a sinner, allowing
myself to scan with worldly eyes

her shabby mack, her cheap red suit,
that truly disastrous nylon blouse
and to wonder, bitchily,
if faith has deprived her of fashion sense.

My fellow congregants are no better:
they tut, they smirk, they bury themselves
in their *Evening Standard*s – anything
but pay attention to the Word.

The truth is, she's doing a lousy job
of spreading it, rushing her Jesus pitch
like an embarrassed English student
clearing her debt with telesales.

I can see humiliation
shining in her cheeks – perhaps
she's made to do it, on pain of losing
whatever celestial credit she has,

or maybe it's love, not fear, which drives her,
a runner's love for the finishing line
fixing her eyes on the middle distance
outside the carriage and over our heads.

She gets off at Dollis Hill, muttering
'God Bless You', without a single backward
glance, lest she turn to salt.
If we ride to Perdition, it won't be her fault.

To the Piped Voice at Westminster Abbey

Granted,
in this place of pilgrimage
nothing could be more appropriate
than a minute's silence,

but when you suggest
that we spend it in prayer
for Those In Power Around the World,
I can't help thinking: why,

in this Imperial glory hole,
where the petrified cast
of the History Syllabus
slumber in their private boxes,
ready for a premium view
on Judgement Day,

while the Innocent Victims,
as a sort of war reparation
are allowed one cramped shelter
outside the West Door,

and the ones who hauled the stones
to raise an Abbey,
who coughed up the taxes
to pay for an Abbey
are left to shiver at the gates

alongside the others:
the starving dead, the plague dead,
the cholera dead, the flu dead
in their plain, dirty winding sheets –

and seeing as how we, the pilgrims,
affluent latecomers, voters and stakeholders
stand before you clutching admission tickets,
which, might I remind you, *we have paid for*,

would it be too much to ask
for us to choose who we pray for?

The Nose on My Face

Someone hopes I don't mind
them asking, but am I – ?
                                 Suddenly
I'm sixteen again, spending
hours in front of my parents' mirror,

holding my hand across the middle
third of my face, admiring
the inoffensive adequacy
of my eyes and mouth, when

they weren't being overshadowed
by my nose, that was so...
What was it about my nose? Did it
have a pushy way of forcing

itself into a room, a vulgar
nose-come-lately, embarrassing
and overdressed? Did it mark
its owner as a fleshy, suburban

princess condemned to a life of shopping
and eating and smothering sons? Was it
transparently over-emotional? Was it
lubricious, dishonest or dirty? Would it

forever spite my face, the kind
of nose that would tell the world that –
                                      Yes,
I say. I am. And someone says
that's funny, they'd never have guessed.

Barton in the Beans

For comfort on bad nights,
open out a map of Middle England

and sing yourself to sleep
with a lullaby of English names:

Shouldham Thorpe, in gentle sunshine,
Swadlincote, in a Laura Ashley frock,

Little Cubley, veins running with weak tea,
Kibworth Beauchamp, praying on protestant knees,

Ashby-de-la-Zouch, saying 'Morning',
Wigston Parva, smiling – but not too widely,

Ramsey Mereside, raising an eyebrow,
Eye Kettleby, where they'd rather not talk about it,

Market Overton, echoing with the slamming doors
of Cold Overton, where teenagers flee every night to their rooms,

screaming that from Appleby Magna to Stubbers Green
they never met a soul who understood.

They never met a soul.
At Barton in the Beans, the rain says *Ssssshhhhh...*

Hummers

At birth perhaps the doctors struck us
like so many tuning-forks,
and this is why our ears are drummed
by a constant rain of things switched on,

and this is why each specialist
will do no more than shrug, and say
that this is a frequency few pick up
and no one can tune out of.

Edinburgh, East of Livingston

Imagine the Old Town
waking up in a rage
and blowing its top,

spitting out pellets
of boiling gum
and blasting stone centuries
into a year of sunsets.

Imagine Edinburgh
becoming its own muddy weather
and hissing into the Firth of Forth.

Imagine the map, melting.

Cold Snap

The lines are down
all the way to Dumfries.
Under my blankets, I hear

the wind trying the door.
Snow breaks on the windows
in muscular waves.

Winter has come
in gardening gloves
to prune dead branches.

John Bellany's *Kiss*

In the sight of God
the jawbones collide.

Here's a pair of lost tongues
and four shifty eyes.

God made kisses from rocks and salt.
God is a cold fish.

Study in Watercolour

Since I became the Other Woman,
my dreams have been as slippery as conscience,
scenes that shift in watercolour

form, unform and run together.
I'm a charcoal mark, ingrained,
the one fixed point in a landscape

that pours like rain through a gutter.
I expect a storm and one appears:
a black cumulus in the shape of a wife.

I brace myself
for a fist like a thunderclap,
but as she grows towards me,

I can see that she is crying
and the tears are washing her face away,
taking the dream with it.

I wake to a voice softer than water:
How could you do this to me?
How could you do it...?

Out with the Muse

The Muse and I
are out on the piss.
He's squeezed up next to me,
with a bottle of Bud
and eyes that follow the barmaid.

He says he likes
a woman who can drink,
but I have to admit
I can't keep up with him –
he's several centuries ahead,
and I'm too slight a vessel
for his kind of inspiration.

I tell him I work in the morning.
'No.' he says, 'No.
You don't need that.
You and me, we're bohemians,
artists, we're above common values.
Have another.
Tell them you're sick.'

I am sick.
I take the last bus home
and fall through the front door,
reaching the bathroom just in time
to bow to Apollo
in his porcelain temple.

The Bowels of Lord Byron

'When dinner has opprest one...'

By eight o'clock
I'm sitting at my desk
and should be working;
instead, I grow pathetic,
sipping my peppermint tea,
(which repeats)

and considering, *inter alia*,
today's misdemeanours,
tomorrow's disappointments,
last month's grief
and a curious sort of question
as to whether the finest feelings
of – George Gordon, Lord Byron, say –
were expressed through his digestion

which seems to have obsessed him,
not to mention his weight –
perhaps that was why
he wrote in the company
of the skulls of Athenian monks:
it was something to aim for,

to be so thin, so free of flesh,
as to escape
the tyrant chains
of his intestines,
a queasy and unerring conscience,
telling him that last night
and the night before that
and on all the nights before,
he had eaten, drunk
and lived too long.

The Whale's Insides

I had intended to drown.
I told him what to do
with his job and jumped,
but he had other plans.

He's booked me onto this cruise
for one. My cabin's hot
and dark. The walls are slimy.
It stinks of rotting fish.

This is the longest night
I've ever spent. I'm no
stranger to insomnia
but this is different:

so still. So quiet. As if
I've fallen down the gap
between two seconds and can't
get free. Time's on remand,

like me. Miles ahead,
I shall be spat into
the light. For now, I'm helplessly
stuck, helplessly moving.

Wisdom at 3 a.m.

I've got stuck again
in the kind of poem
where it's always 3 a.m.
and usually raining.

The wind makes metronomes
of the cypress trees.
Imagine the wind as a feeling,
pulling me inside out
like an umbrella in the storm.

It's a good night for similes.
Maybe it's low blood sugar
or the wide-screen dream
that woke me up,
but I'm feeling profound.

I can see a meaning in this weather,
if I look hard enough –
a heavenly signature
left for exceptional people
like me, to read.

Poor Comet

Poor you.
You never got to be a planet.
You run rings around them
and they ignore it.

You look like a sperm
in pursuit of an egg.
Your white fire
has something desperate about it.

It burns like desire
in the bodies of insomniacs
who've no one to moan at
except for a comet.

Poem to be Thrown Away

'The more I take away,
the bigger it gets.'
GIACOMETTI

He spends his days
squeezing the clay and swearing,
while the sitter and the studio
move in and out of each other,
earth and earthworm.

He can feel the air
sliding its treacly presence
between him and his subject,
who sits minutely
on the farther shore,
looking as if she started to breath out
and forgot to stop,

and under his hands,
the thing he wants to make
is shrinking into itself,
a collapsing star.

The Greyness of Suits

has boxed me in
with swaying walls of pinstripe;
fills my nostrils, blocks the light;

protects the modesty of men,
lending them the stone geometry
of City offices;

surges against me
as we round a bend,
jamming me against the glass,
a pickle crammed into a jar;

drains by degrees
as we grind through the suburbs,
beaching the man with the mud-puddle face
who sags in his seat
like a mollusc out of its shell;

stings my eyes
bitterly, like smoke
as I turn away from him
and step out through the doors;

yawns in the mouth of the tunnel
as man and train recede
down its long, damp oesophagus,
and I mount the station steps
into the ash-grey dusk.

Inner Bloke

When I feel like a drag queen
in tights and heels,
I put that down
to my Inner Bloke.

He's the one
who always has to win,
who comes into his own
in seminars and pub debates.

He knows a lot of facts
and loves to swap them.
There's nothing he won't
turn into a joke,

including me.
He's a bully like that
and needs to put me down.
He's a thwarted thug

and it's all thanks to me,
the body he lives through,
my puny little arms,
that girly way I kick.

Bogeyman

Out of eleven o'clock murk,
a voice:

Got the time, love?

Oh no.
I haven't got the time.
Not for you.
I've been warned about you,

Mr *Got the time?*
Mr *Got a light?*
Mr *Give us a smile*
Mr *Morning, beautiful sweetheart darlin'*

Mr Measuring Eyes
Mr Wolf Whistle
Mr Honk Your Horn
Mr White Van Full Of Hooting Apes

Mr Brainless Yob
Mr Sad Pissed-Up Fart
Mr Dirty Old Should Know Better
Mr Filthy Slimy Perv

Mr SEX FIEND
Mr RECENT SPATE OF ATTACKS
Mr MY FIVE HOUR ORDEAL
Mr LEFT ME FOR DEAD

Mr Don't Cross the Park Alone
Mr Keep The Curtains Closed
Mr Never Sit Like That
Mr Your Knickers Are Showing Through

Mr Be Sensible, Mr Be Quiet
Mr Something To Cry About
Mr Smack You And Send You To Bed
Mr Chopper To Chop Off Your Head

Mr Hangman
Mr Judge
Mr Jailer
Mr Fear.

Thriller

It's on its way,
the just fist in the stomach.

You don't know what you've done
but you've had it coming

ever since the credits
when you opened your curtains

and saw a flock of ragged crows
watching you from the fenceposts.

You must have done it.
Why else would the phone make you jump?

Why else would you avoid
your boss's eyes? And how come

those teenagers giggling on the train
obviously know something?

Wherever you go,
there are eyes just out of shot,

hiding behind a newspaper,
or squinting over a turned-up collar.

Across the reels,
the payoff is stalking you.

Skin

She wakes up peeled, absorbing
stale breath. Without her skin,
she will dissolve in the rain,
so she closes all the windows
and locks the doors. Now
nothing can seep in, nothing
out. The day unravels.
She flickers from room to room
like a series of photographs,
appearing unfocused in doorways
and halfway down the stairs,
with no idea of how she got there.
She cannot collect herself,
not remembering what she keeps
inside, or what to leave out.

Scaling the North Face of Hopkins

It's true: the mind has mountains
and each one of them houses
a hydro-electric power plant.
A hundred billion neurons
are their turbines. Now –

let's say they've all seized up.
They sit like courtiers petrified
by some evil godmother.
The reservoirs are frozen.
An ice age has advanced.

They've repossessed my will.
Getting up without it
is like trying to start a car
when the battery's flat.

They seized my sleep as well
and left behind an invoice
detailing all my faults.
It took all night to read.

They've disfigured the mirror –
I stand petrified
for hours, in front of it,
staring at Medusa.

And my imagination –
they froze it like an asset.
The world's just a tissue of facts
and all I am is ill.

Anyway, back to our mountains:
what we have to do
is to melt the water
and get the turbines moving –
to spring that serotonin

from its locked receptors
and set it flowing freely
thus waking up the neurons.
So, if you take this pill –
I'm sorry, have I lost you?

The Would-Bes

We're not yet human, but we're trying.
We're taking notes, we're taking classes.
We're taking medication. It can
take surgery to straighten kinks

as bad as ours. Sometimes it hurts –
you have to suffer to be human.
Sometimes we cry into our pillows,
but please don't make too much of that:

our tears don't count. We're not yet human
enough to satisfy the judges
that we're not just apes or dummies.
When they're sure they'll let us out

and then we'll live among the humans,
holding hands and pushing buggies,
drinking Coke, doing the things
everybody knows everybody does.

Femenismo

By some standards, I'm a loser.
I've always given in to hunger,

not like the skinny sixth-form queens,
who flexed their iron self-control

and fasted like Olympic gymnasts,
weighing up the competition

like hard men propping up the bar
and willing each other to spill that pint,

giving each other the sidelong looks
that drivers exchange at traffic lights.

Pound the fat and you can wear
your body like a Lonsdale Belt.

That's what we were taught at school –
the rules of swaggering femenismo.

Autodollography

Part One begins
with a rosy, plastic baby
whose tiny tears I wipe
while Mum nurses
my new brother.

Five years on,
a torture scene.
I interrogate the doll
my Grandma gave me,
that Chanukah she died.
I ask why this should be
and pull a cord:
'Please brush my hair,' she says
and other useless things,
so I dismember her,
piece by piece.

This is the start
of a long vendetta.
I declare a War on all Dolls,
the snide, lying bitches,
with their bodies with no openings,
with their eyes that never close,
with their mouths that always smile.
See how the more I scratch them,
throw them, scribble on them,
the more I hurt them
for being stupid,
the more they so despicably smile.

But by Part Two,
I've grown up
and learnt what every girl should know:
that dolls are the perfect decoys
to cover any retreat.
And so we've come to terms.

They answer my phone,
take my place at the office,
sit cross-legged in pubs
laughing at people's jokes.
They're so good at it,
with their even tempers,
their small talk
and those indelible smiles.

No one need ever know
what a nasty girl I am,
not while I hide in my toybox,
upside down and scribbled on.

Primavera

When I look into the mirror
above the loose tomatoes,
I turn the supermarket
into a gothic fresco.

The aisles have multiplied and spread
like brambles re-rooted and gone wild,
the checkouts have forced themselves up,
overnight, like toadstools

and newly hatched, specially reared
under the white striplights,
is a fine selection of babies.
Squirming newborns,
with their apricot scent
and their heads like warm peaches;
teething babies,
dribbling onto their sponge fingers;
walking, helpful babies,
loading glistening tins
into their mothers' trolleys,

overflowing already
like unpruned gardens
with cereals and yoghurt
and family-sized own-brand multipacks,

and every mother
pushing her trolley is a queen
at the head of her own screaming
snotty-nosed state procession.

Staring out of the foreground
there's a young woman
carrying a wire basket
half-full of pasta and apples
and chocolate biscuits.

I take a small step back;
she slips out of the frame.

Mother Chicken Soup

God forbid
her family should starve,
so mother is boiling herself down
for soup,

slicing the carrots
with an upward stroke to the thumb,
rolling perfect *kneidlach*,
mixing up the stock.
After so many years
nothing needs to be measured.

Hasn't she been rehearsing this
for years?
Divided herself, leg and breast,
one, two, three ways
to make three children's mothers?
Put aside her book,
her job, her time?
Taken the food off her own plate
a thousand times?

The oven clock pings.
Time to dissolve her life into theirs,
dive into the broth.

She listens for the other mothers
calling from the pot
then jumps in,
neatly, as she does everything.

Neatly, she has left a note
by the fruitbowl:
'I don't expect gratitude –
only that you should do as much
for your own children.
Turn me up to 150
when you get in. Mum.'

The Old Ladies of Cricklewood

It does no good,
separating old ladies
from homes they've wifed
for fifty years.

They may not remember much –
the date, which pills to take,
the ages of their daughters,
or where they left their husbands last –
but some things they do know:
that this strange hotel is not home,
and that they don't have time
to sit around talking
what with all the shopping to do
and the beds still unmade
and the rubbish not put out.

That's why you see them,
waving out-of-date bus passes
to the drivers in Golders Green,
picking their way down the Vale
with their handbags,
packed with old receipts
and a pair of clean knickers –
because you never know.

An old lady
knows her own front door,
even if it is the wrong colour,
the lock won't work
and there's a stranger
standing behind it.

Deuteronomy

After she had buried her daughter,
she set out for the closing chapter,
a two-week ascent
through the floors of the Royal Free;
she took the lower slopes easily,
moving with slow but definite steps
past the lamps, the trolleys and bedside stands
and on into the upper reaches,
the paler, sickly altitudes
inhabited by light sleepers, rattly breathers,
where words are swallowed up
by the nebulising storms
and thoughts themselves disintegrate
for lack of pressure;
at the last nightfall
she drew the clouds around herself,
leaving the nurses to chart her progress
as a dwindling figure on the pulse oxymeter,
until the hour came
for her to pass through zero,
handing her granddaughters
her wedding band, her empty skin,
stretched like tissue-paper over steel
and her dignity, a family treasure
that cut its shape into our shoulders,
every gem a stone imperative.

Seder Night with my Ancestors

On this night,
my ancestors arrive,
uninvited but expected,
to have their usual word.

They sit around the table
but refuse my offer of food.

I switch the television off
and wait,
the air thickening
with disapproval.

At last I ask them:
What do you want from me?
What have you got to do with me?
Why do you come here, every year
on this night?

And what do they say?

They say:
For this God brought us forth from Egypt?
For this we starved in the desert?
For this we fled the inquisition?
For this we fled the pogroms?

Did we die
refusing unclean meat
for you to fill your fridge with filth?

Did we disguise
our Hebrew prayers
with Christian melodies
so that you could forget them?

For you we did these things?
Do you think the Lord
would have thought you worth saving?

I say that all I want
is to live my life.

Without us you would have no life.

The Whip Hand

She was lighter than the bedclothes
by the time she decided to go,
but first
she had to set me straight:

'Find yourself a nice man, dear,
go out and have fun –
how will you know
if you don't give him a chance?'

So said the woman
who strung my grandfather along
for five years,
two-timing him
while he waited in her mother's kitchen,
playing cards with her brother.

'I never wanted
to marry your Granddad, dear,
but we'd been engaged for three years
and Mum said I had to make my mind up.'

So she did.
Married him and stayed with him,
when he bought them a house
and when he pawned her ring;
when he went off to fight
and when he came home;
when he was promoted
and when he retired;
when their children were married
and when their son died;

until it was unthinkable
that they had ever been anything
but my grandparents,
and together;

until the day he left her
the last last word:

'The man should love the woman
more than the woman loves the man –
that way you have the whip hand, dear.'

The Round-the-World Spoon

Once upon a time,
there was a unique spoon,
with the power to confer honour
upon whichever child drank her soup with it
on a Saturday lunchtime,

for this was the Round-the-World Spoon,
so-called because Granddad
had gone all the way round the world
to earn the right to keep it,

first getting drafted,
sailing South with the 3rd Survey Regiment
to receive an education
in mapping and mathematics,

suffering the trots in Egypt,
flinching from sniper bullets
as he clung to an Italian steeple,
blinking in the gun-engendered brightness
– 'You could've read a book!' –
at the battle of Monte Cassino,

just so he could bear the spoon back,
like a Star of Africa, to Cricklewood
so that, when the time came, small people
could stir Marmite into their soup
with a special spoon,

but even spoons
can lose their magic,
and so it came to pass that, one by one,
the children could no longer see
the Round-the-World spoon,
but only a shallow, battered spoon,
a spoon that dribbled soup
into their laps,

and from that moment,
they had no time for that impractical spoon,
or for stories they'd heard before,
or for his special way of doing algebra,
for his bad jokes, his good war,

and demanded decent, ordinary spoons,
spoons that could do their job,
a spoon for drinking soup with, OK?

Freud on the Station Platform

I arrive early – I'm always early –
but someone is there already:
a familiar old gentleman.
I watch his knuckles whiten
around the handles of his bag,
then I sidle up, respectfully.

'Professor Freud,
don't you think that rail travel
is enough to drive anyone mad?
I mean – maybe the train won't be on time.
Maybe we'll miss it.
Maybe we won't get seats.
And even if it is on time and we do get seats,
the luggage rack might be full
and we'll have to sit for five hours
with our feet on our suitcases.'

He makes
a Mitteleuropean shrug.

'Are you moving as well, Professor?
Do you always feel, when you move,
that until the letters start to arrive,
you're in a sort of deathly limbo?'

His profile asks the middle distance
why they always come to him.

'Then there's that other thing
– do you get it? – vertigo.
I always get it on station platforms.
It's as if the tracks have a magnetic pull.'

He tells the indicator
that he had a patient, in Vienna,
who flung herself on to a suburban railway line,
this being an expression of her wish
to be made pregnant by her father.

There is a long silence.

'Professor Freud, do you think this train
is ever coming?'

He looks at me then,
I see death moving in his jaw.
'Of course it is,' he snaps.

In the Grief Hotel

Every night, on the hour,
you wake to the sound
of someone crying in the next room.

Every morning
they bring you breakfast
along with the bill –

an ever-mounting debt
which traps you here.
You've no choice but to stay
and order lunch,

stay and read the same newspapers
from cover to cover,

stay for afternoon tea
which the staff bring round
on a trolley
for the guests to swallow,
distastefully, like medicine,

stay to eat the usual dinner,
and exchange the usual complaints
about dirt and damp and bad food
and the cost of all this
and how nobody from outside
comes to hear you complain anymore,

to retire to the same room,
where you wash your face
as if it were someone else's,
brush your teeth mechanically,
then sleep too little
or too long,

to wake, on the hour,
to the sound of someone crying
in the next room

to go downstairs in the morning
where they bring you breakfast
along with the bill –

the ever-mounting debt
which traps you here.

Sellotape

Dad died
and three months later
we brought Christmas out again,
an old, fake tree,
shedding its plastic needles.

I broke two nails
in the effort to retrieve
a lost end of Sellotape
as I tried to wrap
the family's presents.

It made a terrible kind of sense,
the closing link
in a paper chain
made of all the unkindnesses
of the world,
like missed buses and stubbed toes,
like tactless remarks
and customers' complaints
and flatmates' dirty dishes.

It was the worst of all losses.
I never cried more
for anything else.
Oh the uselessness of scissors,
the fragility of fingernails,
the pointless waste of Sellotape.

Driving to the Border

Speeding down the autobahn,
ferociously alive,
Dad is as he always is
on family holidays.

It drives us mad
the way he grips the wheel
as if it were the combined necks
of all the drivers
he says he wants to throttle;
the way he splatters insults
out of the window
like machine-gun fire
every time another car
pulls out in front.

Today it's worse than usual.
He wants us to make Austria by six
but the scenery keeps overtaking him.
The faster he chases the border,
the faster it dodges away,
sliding out of sight,
dropping off the map.

From the back seat,
I wish I could tell him
what I've learned:
that not much can be helped;
that there are some things
more disorienting
than this,

like family holidays
with no one speeding,
like a steering wheel
with no one gripping it,
like the unfulfillable wish
to be driven mad
just once more
in just that way.

An Inquest

We knew my father hated change,
so when he died, he left behind
a family of coroners.

We scrutinised the death certificate,
with its coronary argument
and myocardial conclusion

but we had no faith in the testimony
of the white-robed doctors
who only weeks before had wielded

their stainless steel amulets
to ward off the Evil Eye
and declared him fit to be insured.

And no one could claim that he'd neglected
the ritual observances they'd prescribed:
'Cast out sugar. Cast out fat.

Shun unnecessary stress.
Take aspirin to thin the blood
and daily walks to cleanse the breath.'

Clearly, we were asking the wrong
questions: the answers kept wearing off,
like painkillers, or neighbourly sympathy –

but they were all we had. Until,
one month to the hour later,
his namesake, my great-uncle, died

and then we remembered the other prescriptions,
the ones left out of medical textbooks:
'Throw spilled salt over the shoulder.

If you tempt fate, spit.
Never name children after the living,
lest you confuse the Angel of Death.'

So that was all: one careless mistake,
one slip of the pen; an overworked angel
with a clipboard, ticking the wrong name.

The Return

Dad,
I come home
and find you sitting
in every room in the house,
its smell your smell,
as if it were a jacket
you'd only just thrown off,
still warm.

As the house recalls you,
so do I,
resurrecting you
fifty times a day,
in the way you clench my teeth
when something fails to work,
as we prowl in step together
round my room,
hours into the night,
as you fret me into being ready
an hour early for every journey.
As I bite into something undercooked,
I feel you pull
that comical, disappointed face.

You prefer to hide
in better foods:
strong cheese, strong coffee,
anything sweet.
I find myself eating
a whole quarter of wine gums
just to give you
twenty more minutes
of borrowed life.

Maternity

I saw out my father's funeral
a shocked guest in my own home,
drinking and passing
one endless cup of tea,

PG Tips! He'd never let that in the house.

and sat on a low chair
doing nothing for myself,
helpless as a queen bee,

He should've taken better care of himself.

while the living-room buzzed
with kissing cousins and rabbis
and old long-sighted neighbours,

He was so dashing – I remember his red MG.

taking calls and opening doors and feeding me.
First they brought an egg,
then a bagel, for the roundness of life,

Only last week he was telling me a joke.

and then they filed past
planting the seeds
to germinate a father.

He had such knowledge, but he wore it so lightly.

Since then I've eaten for two,
feeling that other person come together
face and voice, inside me.

He was beautiful.

Soon I'll know him, keep him
as thoroughly as any unrequited love,
or longed-for stillborn baby.

Sisyphus' Daughter

A mourner's work is never done.
There was no way to compensate my Dad
for all the small betrayals
of every day I lived
when he did not,
for the indifference of my washing, dressing,
walking, working, talking,
as life on the surface ground on and on
and he was stuck beneath the mud
without so much as a phone
to hear what I was up to.

I couldn't be remembering him all day –
I had enough to think about,
so I resolved to rescue him instead,
packed sandwiches, a handful of change
and my karaoke machine,
and set off for the Underworld,
imagining that when I sang
the dead would flutter to my shoulders
like birds charmed from trees
and I would bring them home.

But when I reached the bank,
I saw my father on the other side,
washing, dressing, walking,
working, talking.
He didn't seem to hear a note –
he had enough to think about.
The afterlife ground on and on.
The work of the dead is never done.

www.ingramcontent.com/pod-product-compliance
Lightning Source LLC
Jackson TN
JSHW020026141224
75386JS00026B/718

* 9 7 8 1 8 5 2 2 4 5 4 0 5 *